Campaigning Online and Winning

How LabourStart's ActNOW campaigns are making unions stronger

By

Eric Lee

&

Edd Mustill

Copyright © 2013 Eric Lee & Edd Mustill
All rights reserved.
ISBN: 1481804448
ISBN-13: 978-1481804448

Preface

Many of the members of unions affiliated to the IUF understand the value of online campaigns. Farm workers, hotel staffers, workers in food manufacturing plants have benefitted over the years from numerous campaigns we've waged using the web, email and new social media.

Our experience with online campaigning goes back to the 1990s and ever since then we have continued improving and learning from experience.

With that experience comes our understanding that online campaigning is just one more tool – often a powerful one – in our toolbox. A web-based campaign is just another tactic, one of many we can employ when trying to support our members. We know that other tools – such as industrial action or other ways of putting a company's brand at risk – can be equally if not more potent.

We've learned over the years that the key to winning online campaigns is in reality not the online campaign itself but rather the determination of the workers on the ground and their unions, combined with the support we can help build for them around the world. That support includes action by IUF affiliates and other unions, often with support from worker-friendly NGOs such as Amnesty International.

LabourStart has pioneered much of this work, as this book shows, and the IUF's on-line beginnings were based on the LabourStart model. Among many other things we've learned is the key role played by mass emailings in building any online campaign. LabourStart's network of over 100,000 online activists is perhaps its greatest achievement – a network which we in the IUF draw upon again and again in addition to our 40,000 strong mailing list to support our members in their struggles.

Today the IUF continues to work closely with LabourStart, promoting our own campaigns, providing the best possible support for our members around the world and supporting other unions' campaigns that are often entrusted to LabourStart.

I hope that this short book with its inspiring stories of workers' victories will encourage all of us to make the best possible use of the technology in order to make our movement more effective, more united and more powerful.

Ron Oswald
General Secretary
International Union of Food, Agricultural, Hotel, Restaurant, Catering, Tobacco and Allied Workers' Associations (IUF)

Contents

Preface by Ron Oswald	iii
Introduction	1
ActNOW: Fighting Victimisation	4
ActNOW: Freeing Prisoners	12
ActNOW: Supporting Strikes	22
ActNOW: What's Disgusting? Union Busting	37
ActNOW: Breaking Lock-outs	43
ActNOW: Taking on the multinationals	47
What We've Learned	52
What You Can Do	55

Introduction

LabourStart didn't invent online campaigning, nor do we make any claim that we're better at this than anyone else. What is unique about LabourStart's experience going back to 1998 is that we exclusively campaign on behalf of, and in partnership with, trade unions.

Back in the 1990s, trade unions had already amassed some experience with online campaigning. The earliest campaigns took place back in the 1980s. But when LabourtStart was launched, we found that many trade unions were struggling to get campaigns right, and about a decade ago we launched our own bespoke system for setting up and running campaigns.

To give an example of how poorly understood was online campaigning by unions, I once showed a class of British union shop stewards an "online campaign" launched by a union in the USA which asked people to send a letter (by post, with a stamp on it) to the CEO of a major, well-known consumer products company.

I asked the shop stewards to try to search online for an email address of the same CEO. Remember - these were ordinary trade union reps, people with no special online skills. It took about 30 seconds before the first one shouted out that they'd found the CEO's email address. So why was the union not bombarding the CEO through email? Why were they using the web to promote a campaign that was no different from one you'd have run back in the 1970s?

The system we set up was very different from the one that exists today, as we learned from experience.

The original ActNOW campaigning system, for example, had no way to "harvest" email addresses of supporters. People would send off their messages, and that was it. Today we know that harvesting those addresses is crucial -- it's what allows us to build a global network of activists. Today, LabourStart has well over 100,000 email addresses on its lists -- the vast majority of them harvested through the online campaigns.

Our original system worked in English only, and today the majority of messages are still sent in English. But a significant and growing minority are sent in Norwegian, French, Spanish, Italian, German, Turkish and other languages. As a result, we now have mailing lists of tens of thousands in those languages.

These should be pretty obvious lessons to have learned, and yet even today we see examples of unions which use tools (sometimes third party tools) that don't allow them to harvest email addresses, or unions which launch global campaigns -- but in only one language.

The stories we tell in this little book are meant to educate and inspire. Running these campaigns over the last decade and more has certainly taught us a thing or two, and inspired us to continue, and to do better.

As you read through the stories, try to remember that these

are always about people, individuals, whose lives can be changed -- and sometimes even saved -- by a successful online campaign.

We've managed to help get trade unionists out of prison, or reinstated at their jobs; we've helped end lock-outs, win strikes, and build stronger unions.

But we've never done that on our own. We've never claimed that we could do that on our own.

It's the partnerships with unions and the work done offline, on the ground, that makes these victories possible.

We don't consider ourselves to be "online activists" and our goal is not some ill-defined "change".

We are first and foremost trade unionists, responsible members of the international labour movement.

Our campaigns, all of them, are designed with one goal in mind: to strengthen that movement, and in doing so to improve the lives of working people.

At the end of this book, we'll try to summarize some of the things we've learned and we'll make some suggestions about how you can help.

If you find this interesting or useful, please let us know -- and more important, let others know. Spread the word in your workplace, your community and your union.

ActNOW: Fighting Victimisation

Across the world, workers are victimised for nothing more than standing up for the rights of themselves and their colleagues. This has always been the case, from the very first struggles for union recognition. But even in workplaces where the union is recognised, and there are agreements covering things like reps' facility time, "troublemaking" individuals are often targeted by management. They know that unions ultimately get their strength from the grassroots, from effective activists on the shop floor.

Many employers are scared of the power of unions, which is why many of them come down so hard on any stirrings of workplace organising. We can't know about, let alone campaign on, every instance of victimisation that goes on. But we can come to the aid of some of our comrades around the world when they need us. Some bosses think they can get away with treating union organisers like criminals, but LabourStart's network of international supporters means we are in a unique position to bring together unionists from around the world to force those employers to think twice. Here are some examples.

UK: Standing up for sacked union reps

In partnership with the National Union of Rail, Maritime, and Transport Workers

In 2010, two union reps on the London Underground, Eamonn Lynch and Arwyn Thomas, faced transparent victimisation.

Eamonn, a Bakerloo Line driver, was sacked, supposedly for following an instruction that turned out to be wrong - but no-one who had given him the instruction was disciplined. A driver who followed a similar instruction a year earlier had only been given a warning. Meanwhile, Arwyn was facing a disciplinary for the way he allegedly behaved towards a manager on a picket line, despite CCTV footage showing that he hadn't done anything wrong during the incident in question.

To the union, it was clear that the actions of the management were motivated by their desire to get rid of some effective workplace activists, at a time when they were trying to push through all sorts of cuts and attacks to working conditions on the tube.

Both members took their cases to employment tribunals, arguing that they had been victimised illegally because of their union activities. Both tribunals found in their favour and ordered that their contracts of employment be upheld.

Despite this, management did not reinstate either of the two. LabourStart publicised the cases of both men from an early stage, and began a campaign targeting Boris Johnson, the mayor of London, who is ultimately responsible for transport in the city.

Eamonn voiced his thoughts on the dispute when nominating LabourStart for the Arthur Svensson prize for international trade union rights in 2012:

Throughout the campaign LabourStart had been wholly supportive in publicising our plight to the wider trade union movement, and I am absolutely convinced that because LabourStart had asked like-minded trade unionists to email the Mayor of London it had a real effect on the outcome.

Over 1000 emails landed on the Mayor's doorstep in a very short space of time. This, without doubt, was instrumental in the reinstatement of both reps. Management doling out punitive discipline to reps and activists cannot be tolerated and must be defended with the whole support of the trade union movement. This in essence is what LabourStart stand for and seek to promote. Solidarity wins. These are the core reasons we become trade unionists. An injury to one is an injury to all.

I am absolutely convinced that coupled with the RMT's industrial action, the widespread coverage given to this dispute by LabourStart was instrumental in getting two reps reinstated. Furthermore, this victory over London Underground led to some ten other reps and activists being reinstated, having disciplinary sanctions reduced or charges against them dropped.

I am deeply indebted to LabourStart for the support and their publicising our victimisation by one of London's biggest employers.

Industrial action had been taken on the individual lines on which Eamonn and Arwyn worked, with little effect. The union decided to broaden out their campaign across the whole London region. In May 2011, the RMT announced ten days of strike action in support of the pair, that would have potentially ground the capital to a halt. The strike was suspended once bosses agreed to reinstate Eamonn. Arwyn won the right to reinstatement after a six month suspension in June.

Ireland: Joanne Delaney reinstated at Dunnes

In partnership with Mandate

Dunnes Stores were known as the Wal-Mart of Ireland because of their intolerant attitude to unions. In the 1980s Dunnes had infamously opposed employees who struck for two and a half years for the right not to handle goods from Apartheid South Africa.

In October 2005, Joanne Delaney was suspended from Dunnes' Ashleaf store in Crumlin for refusing to remove her union badge from her uniform. Joanne had been at the company for four years, and had recently been elected as a shop steward for the Mandate trade union.
The campaign for her release brought together unions and political groups in Ireland, who held meetings and pickets of

Dunnes Stores. The level of public support for Joanne meant that the campaign snowballed and Mandate prioritised it. Joanne won public support from members of the Irish Dail and the British Parliament.

Over 5,000 emails were sent to Dunnes Stores via LabourStart's campaign page. This was a great example of how online campaigns can complement and help to grow an energetic campaign of action on the ground.

PHOTO: Indymedia

In February 2006, Joanne was reinstated. She said: "It was the support and solidarity of fellow trade unionists and of political parties that organised protests throughout the country, and shoppers who use the Ashleaf outlet, who by wearing a Mandate sticker and complaining to management, have done so much to bring about this victory."

Iraq: Jamal Abdul-Jabbar's internal exile stopped

In partnership with the General Federation of Iraqi Workers

In the summer of 2011, Jamal Abdul-Jabbar, the president of the Kirkuk Oil and Gas Workers' Union, was forcibly relocated to a remote location inside Iraq by his employers. In February, he had led a walk-out demanding better health

and safety, and rights for contract workers, and staged a rally outside the HQ of the Northern Oil Company.
The removal of trade unionists to remote locations is a common tactic used by state employers in Iraq, where labour law remains repressive and undemocratic years after the fall of Saddam Hussein. In 2010, after a series of protests at a Basra refinery demanding back pay, the Iraqi Oil Ministry relocated the leaders of the union there to Baghdad. Oil workers are still not allowed to organise in unions that are not tied to the state.

Jamal's cause garnered high profile support from the International Trade Union Confederation (ITUC) and the International Labor Organization (ILO), which embarrassed his government employers into backing down. The General Federation of Iraqi Workers said: "The oil union leader in Kirkuk, thanks to the LabourStart Campaign, has not been relocated, although the risk of being relocated is still hanging over his head."

Victimisation by "internal exile" will remain a constant threat in Iraq until the country's labour laws are changed, but the international workers' movement has shown that we can act quickly to stop it.

New Zealand: SFWU delegate reinstated

In partnership with the Service and Food Workers Union

In 2004, LabourStart appealed to its readers to come to the defence of Andrew Bolesworth, a delegate (shop steward) for the Service and Food Workers Union (SFWU). Bolesworth had been sacked by his employer, a casino in Dunedin, for his union activity.

Some 1,200 messages were sent in the first few days, a large number in LabourStart's early days. The general secretary of Union Network International (UNI) also wrote to the casino management demanding Andrew's reinstatement. The union used a similar strategy to the one Mandate would use in the case of Joanne Delaney, getting members of the public involved by asking casino-goers to wear "I'm union" stickers. The casino even turned away some customers because they were reading a union leaflet.

Soon after the campaign got up and running, Andrew got his job back.

We know what a galvanising effect a victory at one workplace can have on other workers who have been kept in the loop. The union wrote, "Thank you to everyone who sent emails, wrote letters of support, signed the petitions, turned up at the pickets - the members at Dunedin are really energised about unionism after a brief introduction and a big win."

Pakistan: Hotel shamed into re-hiring union president Haji Gul Hassan

In partnership with the International Union of Foodworkers (IUF)

Haji Gul Hassan was President of the Quetta Serena Hotel Workers' Union. In 2005, he was dismissed from his job. When he tried to approach the hotel to deliver a grievance letter, he was beaten by security guards.

After an online campaign, Haji was reinstated. According to the IUF, "over 750 people from around the world responded ... Coupled with your messages of concern to the management and owners of the Quetta Serena Hotel, the local union was able to campaign effectively and successfully in reinstating their union president, Brother Haji Gul Hassan, and two other union activists. The union asked the IUF to convey their heartfelt thanks to all those who sent messages of support. The union also stated that the email messages made a visible difference to the campaign, with the management and owners clearly affected by the international response."

This shows that even a relatively small campaign can win in some workplaces, like the hotel industry, where employers are very concerned with their public image. We can use international outrage and the threat of a bad name to bring pressure on these employers.

PHOTO: IUF

ActNOW: Freeing Prisoners

In many parts of the world, our brothers and sisters face much more extreme forms of repression. Those who have the misfortune to live under a dictatorial regime often face imprisonment, torture, and even death for sticking to their principles. Often, such governments set up so-called "unions" which are controlled by the state, and merely act to police workers and make sure discontent goes nowhere. In these circumstances, activists who try to set up genuine independent unions are a thorn in the side of such organisations, and the government.

Many of the people we mention in this section have spent their entire working lives facing persecution, simply for trying to organise - and succeeding. The labour movement has always been on the side of democracy against dictatorship. Unions continue to be at the forefront of the struggle for democracy, particularly in the Arab world at the moment, where they face threats from old autocracies and Islamist organisations alike. Organised workers played a big role in toppling Mubarak in Egypt and Ben Ali in Tunisia, and since the beginning of the revolutions they have been out on the streets again and again to make sure workers' rights are not sidelined.

Sometimes it seems like states can be all-powerful. But we know that even the most repressive governments can be forced to back down when the international labour movement moves into action.

Bahrain: Free Mahdi and Jalila!

PHOTO: Maryam Abu Deeb

In partnership with the Education International

Mahdi Abu Dheeb and Jalila al-Salman are the president and vice-president of the Bahrain Teachers' Association (BTA). They were arrested in 2011 for their role in the pro-democracy movement which had begun its mass protests at the Pearl Roundabout on 14th February. Mahdi Abu Deeb was at the roundabout almost every day. His daughter Maryam told al-Jazeera: "He would leave home in the morning and come back late at night. If he wasn't at Pearl, he was meeting people about schools."

The BTA called two strikes in February and March 2011, in protest at the government's violent treatment of the protesters, many of whom were students. Mahdi called for students to join in an education strike, and for parents not to send their children to schools during the strikes.

On 29th March, Jalila was arrested by 40 police officers at her house in Manama. A week later, Mahdi was arrested at his brother's home. Both activists were subjected to solitary confinement and beatings while in custody. Jalila told journalists:

"They used a black rubber hose to beat me. One cell had dried blood on the walls and hook in the ceiling. It was a place for torture. They kept me for eight days in a freezer. They wanted me to sign a confession. I don't how I survived."

In September, they were both tried by military court and found guilty of planning the violent overthrow of the regime, although no evidence of this has ever been presented. Mahdi was sentenced to ten years in prison, and Jalila got a three year sentence.

PHOTO: MENA Solidarity

Education International (EI) and teaching unions around the world responded quickly to the ill-treatment of the

BTA leaders. LabourStart helped EI run two online campaigns for the release of the pair. The second campaign was launched in October 2012, after the convictions of the pair had been upheld by a civilian court. It got thousands of responses within a few hours, and became one of LabourStart's largest ever campaigns, with 11,000 responses.

> *I was only released because of solidarity and international pressure. I don't want to go back to prison, but you have to fight for your rights. They will not come to you - you have to go and fight for them.*
>
> **Jalila al-Salman**

Jalila was released from prison on 25th November, but Mahdi Abu Deeb remains serving a reduced five year sentence. EI and LabourStart continue the campaign to free Mahdi.

Egypt: Charges dropped against union leader Kamal Abbas

In partnership with the International Trade Union Confederation (ITUC)

Kamal Abbas is a veteran of workers' struggles in Egypt. Long before the fall of Hosni Mubarak, as a welder in a Cairo steelworks, he helped to lead an illegal strike of 17,000 workers against the regime.

Abbas founded the Centre for Trade Union and Workers' Services (CTUWS) to raise the banner of independent workers' organisation, outside of the 'official', state-

PHOTO: Hossam el Hamalawy

controlled, Egyptian Trade Union Federation (ETUF). The CTUWS helped bring together emerging independent unions in the years between the Mahalla general strike of 6th April 2006 and the overthrown of Mubarak in 2011.

In February 2012, Abbas was convicted in absentia by an Egyptian court of "insulting a public officer." This referred to an incident in Geneva during the annual International Labour Conference in 2011, which Abbas attended as a guest of the International Trade Union Confederation.

Abbas interrupted Ismael Fahmy, the acting president of the ETUF and an embodiment of the remnants of the Mubarak regime which still cling to positions of power. He questioned what right the ETUF, one of the pillars of the old regime, had to claim to represent Egyptian workers to the ILO.

LabourStart ran a high profile international campaign with the ITUC for the charges to be dropped, which got nearly

7,500 responses. The ITUC issued public appeals to unions around the world, and to the ILO, supporting Abbas's view of Fahmy and the ETUF.

The CTUWS appealed the conviction, challenging the sentence by using the ILO's conventions. As a delegate to the conference, Abbas should not have been prosecuted for the content of his speeches. And, as the leader of what is supposedly a union federation, Fahmy should not have been counted as a "public officer."

On 25th November 2012, the court in Helwan finally quashed Abbas's six-month prison sentence. This was a big victory for the independent labour movement in Egypt, at a time when it was coming under new pressure from the Muslim Brotherhood-led government of President Morsi, who was trying to tie unions to his own party, and make it impossible for them to challenge his actions in the courts.

Through organisations like CTUWS and the Egyptian Federation of Independent Trade Unions, organised labour has become a major player in the Egyptian revolution. It was a wave of workers' strikes and sit-ins that finally forced Mubarak out in 2011, and now unions are at the forefront of the fight for a secular, democratic state.

When LabourStart founder Eric Lee interviewed Kamal Abbas in London in 2011, the Egyptian said, "the revolution succeeded in removing the dictatorship — but we are only half-way to a democratic state and in transition to building independent unions which are a basis of a more socially just and democratic system."

Iran: Mansour Osanloo freed

In partnership with the International Transport Workers Federation (ITF)

The years 2004-6 saw a massive wave of industrial struggles in Iran, involving workers from copper works to car plants to teachers in schools. After years of repression by the theocratic regime, the labour movement in Iran was returning to political life with militancy and confidence.

Bus drivers in Tehran were just one of the groups who formed a new union. Despite threats from the regime's thugs, thousands of them came together to elect representatives. Mansour Osanloo was chosen as the union's president.

The union drew up demands for recognition, wage parity with other public employees, and provision of uniforms from the employer. In the autumn of 2005 they began an imaginative campaign of disobedience, including driving with their lights on all day, and refusing to collect fares from passengers.

On 22nd December 2005, Mansour Osanloo and fourteen of his comrades were arrested. The union responded with a strike on all Tehran's buses in January, during which over 1,000 more arrests were made. The strike effectively shut down the Iranian capital, which is dependent on busses.

The International Transport Workers Federation responded with a global day of action on 15th February 2006. In the following days, most of the activists were released from Evin prison. Osanloo was released after almost six months of solitary confinement.

One union member said: "On the internet, we are constantly updated on support from workers in other countries. We will keep hold of these new contacts, since they are very dear to us."

So they would prove to be. Osanloo, and other union members, were rearrested several times in the following years. In November-December 2006 he was held for another month before being released on bail, and subsequently allowed to travel to Europe for conferences of the ITF and ITUC. He said to the ITF:

"Perhaps our government may not recognise us yet but it's important that the ITF and trade unions around the world recognise us. We are proud to have your support."

On his return to Iran he was imprisoned yet again. Due to a lack of medical treatment, his eyesight began to seriously deteriorate. LabourStart ran an online campaign for his release, and it became one of our largest, as the courageous story of the formation of a democratic, independent union in Iran inspired trade unionists around the world.

Osanloo was released in June 2011, after four years of pressure and campaigning. ITF general secretary David Cockcroft said, "He is free because trade unionists around the world demanded justice."

The bus workers' union contines to be at the forefront of Iran's re-emergent labour movement. The fight to defend its members, like imprisoned treasurer Reza Shahabi, from persecution continues.

Morocco: Said El Hairech freed

In partnership with the International Transport Workers Federation

Said El Hairech, General Secretary of the Moroccan Merchant Mariners, was arrested in June 2012 on trumped-up charges relating to national security. His real crime had been to organise and win better conditions for dockers and seafarers in the western Mediterranean. He had been involved in securing rights for Moroccan sailors stranded in European ports when the Comarit-Comanav ferry company went bankrupt.

Our online campaign gained over 5,600 supporters. Meanwhile, the International Transport Workers Federation organised solidarity protests around the world. Said was freed on 1st October.

When I was in jail I knew the whole world was behind me. I thought, they cannot resist such a campaign.

Said El Hairech

El Salvador: Atilio Jaimes Perez released

In partnership with the Solidarity Center

Atilio Jaimes Pérez, secretary general of SELSA, a union at a LIDO factory in El Salvador, was arrested outside the factory by the National Civil Police for allegedly making death threats. Management had called him outside under the pretence of entering negotiations around an ongoing strike, then attempted blackmail by offering to withdraw the accusation if the strike was called off.

Atilio was released 17 days and 1,542 names later.

Bangladesh: Mehedi Hasan released

In partnership with Labour Behind the Label

Mehedi Hasan was arrested in January 2008 at Zia International airport while boarding a flight to Bangkok. Mehedi was working in the field for the Workers' Rights Consortium, a US-based group working for universities and colleges to monitor working conditions in factories that make clothes bearing their names.

Mehedi was released soon after the online campaign got up and running. Unions and rights groups still have many concerns about the freedom of labour activists in Bangladesh, and the textile industry there remains notoriously dangerous.

ActNOW: Supporting Strikes

Unions often find that their demands, however reasonable and justified, fall on the deaf ears of management or the government. Such intransigence from employers can mean that a dispute gets stuck in the mud. One way that a union can try to break the deadlock is to call for international solidarity and material support. Some of the most high profile disputes in the history of the workers movement have been kept alive with the help of brothers and sisters in other countries. The French CGT gave truckloads of food to the British miners in the strike of 1984. Going back even further, Australian dockers sent money to their British counterparts during the seminal dock strike of 1889.

International support is particularly necessary if a dispute has been dragging on for a long time. It keeps up the morale of striking workers and reminds them that they are part of a global class fighting for the same things right across the world. It can also help to amplify a dispute if the eyes of global public opinion are fixed on a particular place, as was the case during the 2012 London Olympics.

UK: Cleaners fight for pay justice

In partnership with the National Union of Rail, Maritime, and Transport Workers

As the London 2012 Olympics approached, we heard more and more about how much money the games were going to bring into the UK economy. Transport workers in London, who face difficult busy conditions at the best of times, rightly asserted that they deserved a bonus for working during the games, when in excess of a million extra commuters were expected. The RMT managed to secure Olympic bonuses for its drivers and station staff, as did Unite for London's bus drivers.

Cleaners on the London Underground, who work for contractors like Initial and Carlisle, and earn a base rate close to the minimum wage, wanted to get in on the action too. With the eyes of the world on Britain's capital, the RMT approached LabourStart to help them organise a "cyber picket" of the Mayor of London's office – and over 5,000

PHOTO: CitizenBarnet blog

RMT is delighted to have linked up with our friends at LabourStart to launch this important global campaign in support of the tube cleaners fight for workplace justice while London is the centre of worldwide media attention. No doubt it will help us apply maximum pressure to the Mayor, TfL [Transport for London] and the cleaning companies to end this scandal of poverty pay on London Underground.

Bob Crow, RMT General Secretary

people responded.

The RMT's campaign for better conditions for cleaners is ongoing, and they are now focusing on winning the London Living Wage from contractors like Carlisle on national rail routes. Meanwhile, the revolt of cleaners in London continues, as IWW and IWGB members have won pay rises at John Lewis stores in the capital, and Unison cleaners at the University of London press on with their "3 Cosas" campaign for sick pay, holidays, and pensions.

Botswana: Public sector workers strike strengthens labour movement

In partnership with Public Services International

A huge public sector strike of 100,000 workers began in Botswana on 18th April 2011. Workers wanted a 16% pay rise, after three years of getting nothing.

The government's response was to sack hundreds of essential workers, and set the police on striking workers in increasingly violent attacks.

Embarrassingly for the government of Botswana, the online campaign was launched at the same time at the ILO's annual International Labour Conference. Public Services International said:

"The launch of the campaign was timely and caused a stir during the ILC , which led to (failed) attempts to discredit the information in the text amongst ILC delegates. I am sure that the campaign was useful in facilitating our lengthy meeting with a 6 people strong government delegation during the ILC. I believe it also played a useful part in facilitating further meetings between PSI affiliates and other unions belonging to the federation BOFEPSU and the ruling party, from which we hope progress will result."

The union leaders eventually accepted a 3% pay rise from the government, but the strike is widely seen as a landmark development in the increasing power of the labour movement in Botswana.

Australia: Sydney Hilton workers win payouts

In partnership with the Liquor, Hospitality, and Miscellaneous Workers' Union (now United Voice)

In late 2002, the Sydney Hilton Hotel announced that it was closing for 18 months, in order to undergo a $400 million refurbishment. Nearly 500 hotel staff were told that they would be laid off, with no guarantee that they would get their jobs back when the place reopened. To add insult to injury, Hilton used a loophole in the law to offer just eight weeks redundancy pay, half the usual amount offered in Australia. The Liquor, Hospitality and Miscellaneous Workers Union (LHMU), which represented the workers, was frozen out of discussions altogether.

The LHMU approached LabourStart with a view to running an ambitious international, online campaign. The hotel manager's inbox was flooded by hundreds of protest emails, making it impossible for him to carry on working. After a few days, he contacted the LHMU, but only to ask them to stop bombarding him with messages! Over 3,000 were sent in all, which made the campaign one of LabourStart's largest up to that date.

The protest not only made it clear that people were angry with the actions of the Sydney Hilton management, but also that they would contact their local Hilton and explain what was going on. This is the sort of damage to the brand that multinationals in the service industry can't afford to let get out of hand.

Hilton agreed to open negotiations, but there were, of course, sticking points. The union wanted four weeks redundancy pay for every year of service, and first-preference to ex-employees for rehiring when the hotel opened again. The workers decided to stage a 24 hour strike. A coalition was brought together, including Filipino and Fijian community groups, reflecting the diversity of this mainly migrant workforce. These groups helped get the word out to other workers in those communities not to cross picket lines.

> *Sydney's 500 Hilton Hotel workers have won a magnificent victory, and they owe it to the more than 3,000 people from around the world who joined a cyber-picket line, sending protest e-mails to the Hilton Hotel chain's top executives.*
>
> **LMHU**

The strike rally was addressed by members of many of Australia's unions, and via video by Rev. Jesse Jackson from the US.

On November 1st, with the campaign just seven weeks old, the LHMU announced a victory. Redundancy pay was increased substantially, and also paid to casual workers, who were originally offered nothing. Hilton also agreed to recognise the union.

This cyber picket line was, of course, only backing up the real physical picket line of the hotel staff themselves. The two of them made a powerful combination that was able to win a much better deal for the Sydney Hilton workers.

USA: Material solidarity at Azteca Tortillas

In partnership with the United Electrical Workers

Over the winter of 2002-3, members of UE Local 1159 found themselves engaged in a long, bitter strike at the Azteca Tortillas factory in Chicago. Azteca were refusing to negotiate a fair contract with the union.

Federal authorities had issued Azteca with numerous citations for health and safety violations. According to the workers, protective equipment was lacking, and bleach used in the production process was causing severe rashes and burns.

In April 2002, a large majority of Azteca workers voted to leave their company-controlled  union and join the United Electrical Workers. The company refused to bargain with the union in good faith, simply proposing swinging cuts to working conditions. In September, the strike began for a fair contract.

LabourStart began a campaign with a difference. As well as asking people to send off letters of protest, we also asked for money for the workers' Christmas fund. This helped them by Christmas presents for their children, as the strike dragged on through the winter. The amount of money donated wasn't a fortune, but it was invaluable. It showed that other workers around the world, who had probably never even heard of Azteca Tortillas and were not even aware of the dispute, were willing to put their hands in their pockets and help out their brothers and sisters in America.

Azteca finally agreed to accept federal mediation in February 2003. In May, the workers returned to work, after a seven month stoppage during which not one of the strikers had gone back.

Azteca agreed to settle charges charges filed by UE Local 1159 that it illegally threatened to fire workers for union activity and that it violated their rights though intimidating interrogations and surveillance.

UK: The Fremantle dispute - A 21st century free speech fight

In partnership with Unison

By 2007, like an increasing number of their colleagues, low-paid care workers in Barnet, north London, had been outsourced from the council to a new employer. In Barnet, this was the Fremantle Trust. As is often the case with outsourcing, the workers

PHOTO: @skinnyvoice

found themselves doing the same job but for long hours, fewer holidays, and less sick pay. Unison estimated that some workers could lose up to 30% of their pay. When they decided to strike against this, one of their shop stewards, Andrew Rogers, was victimised by Fremantle.

On the face of it, this wasn't necessarily a campaign that LabourStart would get involved in. It was a very localised dispute, where we usually promote those that have a more obvious international angle. It didn't seem like it would get much of an international response.

But the issued raised by the Fremantle dispute were global. After all, here was a low-paid workforce of mostly women, fighting against privatisation. And their local union branch was keen to use the internet to gather support for their struggle.

Fremantle's response to the campaign was an unusual one. Instead of backing down or ignoring it, they decided to try to get it shut down. Angry at having their actions challenged, they wrote to LabourStart demanding that we stop our "potentially libellous" campaign. Simultaneously, they also wrote to our internet service provider, who then gave us a day to remove the campaign page, or else have our entire site shut down!

Unison sent a letter to the ISP explaining that this was an industrial dispute, and that what they had heard and were acting on was just one side of the story. Unfortunately, this got no response. We were facing losing our entire website.

Before the deadline passed, we closed down the Fremantle campaign page. But just two hours later it was back, on another ISP based in Australia, with a brand new domain name: wewillnotbesilenced.org.

Fremantle's attempt to shut us up had massively backfired. Trade unionists around the world were outraged that a "non-profit" organisation could have such a disregard for freedom of speech. The campaign generated over 12,000 messages, our biggest at the time, thousands of them coming in the days immediately after Fremantle's blunder. Soon after this, the ISP contacted us admitting that our campaign material could not be considered defamatory.

The incident generated a huge amount of interest in the campaign from people who otherwise wouldn't have heard about it. No-one has since tried to threaten to shut down one of our online campaigns in such a bald-faced way.

Unfortunately, Barnet Council have not learned the lessons from catastrophic outsourcing. Their "One Barnet" programme has recently seen as much as 70% of the council's services packaged and sold off to the private sector, so there are many more battles to be fought yet.

Philippines: The Hacienda Luisita massacre

The Hacienda Luisita is a huge sugar plantation in the Philippines, owned by the powerful Cojuangco family, which as long been part of the country's political elite.

Plantation workers belonging to the ULWU and CATLU unions went on strike at noon on 6th November 2004, demanding the reinstatement over over 300 unionists who had been sacked by the owners. The strike took the form of an occupation, and pickets built barricades around the plantation.

Ten days later, soldiers and police attacked a picket line, killing seven workers and injuring hundreds more.

PHOTO: Asian Peasants Coalition

The dispute ran on for another year, until December 2005, when ULWU won many of its demands for the payment of wages and benefits. Some of the victimised workers were rehired, and others were given retirement packages.

This is an example of a campaign launched when a dispute was already quite old, but one which still helped get results.

Norway: The successful campaign that was never launched

Here, LabourStart correspondent Espen Loken describes a campaign in 2010 which won before it was even launched!

Norway and the Scandinavian countries are probably the part of the world where the trade unions are strongest, where most workers, both blue and white collar, are members of a union, where wages are decent, where working conditions on the whole are acceptable, where trade union rights are respected by both the Government and by most employers.

But even if we are fairly well off in Norway and Scandinavia – it is also important to defend our rights. The trade unions have fought for these rights for more than 100 years – and we can lose them if we don't care, if we don't fight all attempts to weaken them.

LabourStart has become a success in Norway and elsewhere because we do not stand outside of the labour movement, doing campaigns for the workers. We are a part of the union movement family, even if we are, and shall continue to be, independent as an organization. LabourStart in Norway has for years shown itself to be a good and reliable source for news about workers' issues. The unions know that.
The key points here are:

1) The campaign was planned in close cooperation with the affected workers and unions, not from the outside,

2) The campaign was a part of an overall strategy, including many weapons, like striking and demonstrations on the ground, and

3) Success must not be measured on how many e-mails are sent, but on the result for the workers. In fact this online campaign was never launched – yet I will say it was one of LabourStart's successful campaigns. How can I say that?

This campaign was about a small company out in the middle of nowhere – or in a small town in the middle of Norway – with 60 workers making working clothes – owned by one family. The owner refused to enter into a collective agreement with the workers. The company was his, and he wanted to rule alone.

Consequently the workers had to go on strike in late 2010. They had picket lines every day outside the factory. The owner did what he could to weaken the union and the strikers, and some were even pressured to back off before the strike started. The situation was quite deadlocked – half the workforce was on strike, the rest were working.

In this situation I offered to make them an online campaign. Even if some of the union leaders in the district knew LabourStart and online campaigns, most of the strikers had no experience, and were skeptical for many reasons. Would it be worth putting effort into it? What about legal issues?

So we had discussions. I discussed with the national unions and with the local unions, and they had meetings with the strikers. We ended up with a strategy of stepping up the pressure, of which an online campaign was going to be a part.

The first part of stepping up the pressure was demonstrations where union activists came in buses from around the country to show their solidarity.

Secondly, the transport workers union declared that they would block all deliveries to and from the company. According to Norwegian law such sympathy actions must be declared 14 days before they can be executed. It was even postponed for a period because the owner took the transport workers to court, where he eventually lost.

Thirdly, we would launching an online campaign at the same day as the transport workers blocked the deliveries.

In the meantime we prepared the online campaign. We made sure the information was 100% correct so that the owner had no excuse for taking us to court. We agreed with the workers on a target; on the e-mail addresses that should receive the protest e-mails, and alternative e-mail addresses in case the company managed to stop the e-mails. We talked about how to engage local people and union members around the country in the campaign, and made sure LabourStart was ready to launch the campaign globally.

Everything was settled and ready. I just had to push the button.

Then, the day of stepping up to this next level with sympathy actions and online campaigning, the owner of the company gave up. He declared that he was ready to make collective agreements both with the blue and white collar workers. So I never pushed the button. Even so, I say that this was a successful LabourStart campaign.

Why?

1. We have to be a part of the union movement, working close with the unions – not stand on the outside.

2. Online campaigning may be a powerful tool – but must be combined with activity on the ground. The battle is not virtual – it's very physical.

3. The most important is that the workers win – the number of e-mails is not important in itself.

In this case the workers won, and LabourStart also got many new friends in Norway, which will help us in later campaigns.

ActNOW: What's Disgusting? Union Busting!

Sometimes employers will, simply and baldly, try to break a union. They will refuse recognition, withdraw contracts, and sack workers en masse just to try to get the union out of "their" workplace. This not only violates the right to organise, but often goes against various labour laws in different countries, as well as the International Labor Organization's core conventions. Employers hope that one big defeat will force the union out of their workplace for good, and allow them to dispense with collective bargaining altogether. Some corporations take pride in making an "anti-union" reputation for themselves.

But it's not just corporations who are union busting. Too often, governments try to break the power of public sector unions among their own employees too – think of the Wisconsin dispute in the USA for a recent example. Struggles for the most basic rights are often the most bitter and protracted, and LabourStart is there to mobilise international support.

India: Suzuki workers fight for union recognition

In partnership with the International Metalworkers Federation (now part of IndustriALL)

Workers at three Suzuki plants in India started a sit-down strike on 7th October 2011, demanding the reinstatement of locked-out contract workers. Two days later, workers at Suzuki Motor Cycles Ltd were fired upon. The Indian Labour Ministry backed the company and called the strike illegal. The company then sacked dozens of workers for their involvement in the strike.

PHOTO: Maruti Suzuki Workers Union

After talks with the union and the government, the company backtracked and reinstated 64 of the sacked workers. Thirty other suspended workers received compensation from the company, which caused some bad feeling among others who saw this as a pay-off or a sell-out. The remaining workers reiterated their demand for an independent union.

This new union, the Maruti Suzuki Workers' Union, was recognised by the company, until the riots at Manesar in

July 2012, which were used as a reason to derecognise it once again. The struggle at Suzuki continues.

Italy: Fiat de-registers a union for refusing to sign up to its deal

In partnership with FIOM-CGIL and the International Metalworkers Federation (now part of IndustriALL)

In 2011, Fiat effectively de-recognised Fiom-CGIL, one of the largest unions in Italy, because the union had refused to sign up to a new "agreement" which attacked workers' rights and conditions.

Nearly 8,000 people worldwide signed up to the appeal to restore union freedom at the company. Fiom said the campaign was greatly appreciated in Italy, giving their members the sense of belonging to a "workers' world" and introducing them to tools for international solidarity that they were not familiar with before.

Thousands of Italian workers participated in the campaign, and since then have participated in many other LabourStart campaigns as well.

Fiom's legal challenges for the right to representation are still ongoing and have had successes. In June 2012 a court in Naples ordered Fiat to re-hire 145 Fiom members.

Campaigns like this show governments and bosses that the working class can move into action globally to fight the union-busting designs of multi-national companies.

Canada: Canada Post workers fight back-to-work law

In 2011, LabourStart teamed up with the Canadian Union of Postal Workers to fight the Harper government's plan to force them away from the negotiating table and undercut their collective bargaining rights. The LabourStart campaign gathered nearly 14,000 names in a dozen languages, making it one of our largest. This is what the union had to say:

CUPW wants to thank LabourStart for this campaign. It buoyed our spirits, made it clear that for many people back to work legislation is unacceptable, and put pressure on the Minister. Although the back to work legislation was ultimately passed, the help and support from LabourStart made a difference for CUPW members. Even though we have been ordered back to work, our fight is not over. CUPW's members heads are held high and we will continue to work for respect, dignity, and a sharing of the benefits. We will demand our rights in the workplace, and continue to work with allies for fairness for postal workers and to regain our right to free collective bargaining. We will work with our allies for justice locally, nationally, and internationally. We are proud of the struggle we have waged and are determined tocontinue it. CUPW looks forward to continuing to work with LabourStart.

Ecuador: Public sector workers bring government to the table

In partnership with the Public Services International

With just over 2,000 responses, this is an example of how even a smaller campaign can be useful to unions.

On 28th October 2011, the Ecuadorian Labour Ministry sacked over 3,000 public sector workers, some of whom were removed from their workplaces forcibly by the police.

According to Public Services International: "Combined with other actions by PSI, [the online campaign] generated a useful response from the government – a detailed letter of response, which at one stage the government was also copying to all those who had signed the on-line campaign. The response itself was rather unsatisfactory, but useful to our affiliates in terms of media work and keeping up the pressure. The President's office has also asked the labour minister to explore the possibility of a meeting with PSI representatives in order to discuss matters further."

Mexico: Global week of action for union rights

In partnership with the International Metalworkers Federation (now part of IndustriALL)

This campaign was launched around a global week of action in February 2011, protesting against ongoing attacks by the government of Mexico on the country's trade union movement. Many unions were facing persecution, including the miners, electrical workers, university workers, and telephone workers, and they turned to the international trade union movement to help.

During the week of action, 50,000 people rallied in 40 countries in protests organised by global unions, and 3,677 letters of protest were sent off via LabourStart. The action gave confidence to Mexico's union movement, and led to the release of union leader Juan Linares, who had been in prison for two years.

A campaign like this one shows that getting people active around a big general issue – in this case the general fight for union rights in Mexico – can get concrete results on the ground.

ActNOW: Breaking Lock-outs

The lock-out has been a tactic of bosses since the labour movement first began. A lock-out is a form of blackmail – refusing work to people unless they come back on the bosses' terms. Lock-outs often last weeks and months, particularly if the employer is determined and digs their heels in. That's why international solidarity is so important. The workers recognised this during the famous Dublin lock-out of 1913-14, which lasted for over six months and brought some working-class families to the brink of starvation. Union activists James Connolly and Jim Larkin embarked on tireless speaking tours outside Ireland to whip up moral and physical support for the workers.

At LabourStart, we don't have the resources to put on speaker tours or send food parcels, but we do have the capacity to galvanise thousands of trade union activists into taking action to end lock-outs. Here are some examples of employers who have been brought back to the table, and been forced to make concessions.

Turkey: Fighting for justice at GEA

In partnership with the International Metalworkers Federation (now part of IndustriALL)

Sixty-two members of the Turkish metalworkers' union Birlesik Metal-IS were locked out in July 2011 for allegedly taking illegal strike action ... during their lunch breaks! The move seemed like a deliberate ploy from the bosses, a subsidiary of the German-owned GEA group, to damage the union's ability to renegotiate its collective agreement. Despite its own reports stating that no such strike action had taken place, the company refused to meet with the workers and called police in to the factory.

International unions like the IMF and ITF moved into action, and an online campaign was launched. Participants in the second annual LabourStart Global Solidarity Conference held in Istanbul joined an international delegation at the workers' picket line on 18th November 2011 (pictured on the cover of this book). That month, a Turkish court ruled that four workers dismissed at GEA should be reinstated. In December, German trade unionists held actions at GEA offices in Düsseldorf, and sent delegations to the picket in Turkey.

GEA eventually agreed to talk to the Turkish union and the IMF, noting the large volume of protest messages they had received.

New Zealand: Hospital workers appeal for solidarity

In partnership with the Service and Food Workers Union

Cleaners, kitchen staff, and orderlies belonging to the Service and Food Workers Union found themselves locked out in July 2007. Most were workers who made minimum wage or not much higher. Their bosses were trying to force them out of a national framework for negotiations which covered other workers in the sector.

This campaign ran for just a week before the company was forced to come to the negotiating table on 24th July.

USA: Seven-week lockout at San Francisco hotels

In partnership with UNITE-HERE

In September 2004, members of UNITE-HERE local 2 in San Francisco working in four of the city's most prestigious hotels went on strike. Bosses responded with a lock-out, which was extended to other hotels. The lockout lasted 53 days.

The dispute cost the hotel between $50 million and $100 million. In November, the employers relented, the lock-out ended, and negotiations began. Gavin Newsome, the mayor of San Francisco who had been sympathetic to the hotel workers, cited negative publicity as one of the reasons for the hotel owners agreeing to negotiate.

Local 2 continues to organise workers in the city's big hotels, and has been involved in several high profile disputes since 2004.

ActNOW: Taking on the Multinationals

The fight for workers' rights has always been a global one. Now, more and more, we see individual disputes that take on a global dimension. After the Chinese and US militaries, many of the world's biggest employers are multinational corporations. Think Walmart (2.1 million employees), McDonalds (1.9 million), and Foxconn (1.2 million).

If you're a worker in almost any industry, there's a decent chance that your real bosses, the company that owns your company, are thousands of miles away. Your supply chain probably includes companies and workforces in several different countries. There's a good chance that, whatever your bosses are trying to do to you, they've tried it with someone else in the past, or will in the future. So it makes sense to appeal across borders for those workers to show solidarity.

That's where LabourStart comes in. We can mobilise union activists across the world to protest against the role of multinationals and governments in their own country and abroad. Here are a few examples of campaigns we've helped to run with a real global scope.

Indonesia: G4S workers win their jobs back

In partnership with UNI global union

In 2005, 150 security officers at Group 4 Securicor were sacked after organising a strike. LabourStart ran two campaigns at the request of UNI, neither of which got much of a response initially, with only a few hundred people sending messages.

Indonesian courts ruled the sackings illegal, but the company still would not rehire the workers, so the following year they began a sit-in at the company's headquarters in Jakarta. This time, LabourStart's online campaign produced over 6,000 messages of protest and solidarity with the workers.

> *We have heard from the company how much the involvement of unions and individuals from around the world has infuriated them. They thought they could ignore our rights and our laws without any consequences, but instead they found themselves in an international spotlight. We want to express our thanks to LabourStart, and particularly to the more than 6,000 people who wrote emails demanding that the company respect our rights and our country's laws.*
>
> **Timboel Siregar, Association of Indonesian Labour Unions**

In July, as a result of their more militant tactics. the workers were finally reinstated. This goes to show that a change in circumstances on the ground can have a big effect on the success or otherwise of an online campaign. Effective online campaigns have to be able to respond to the actions workers are taking in the real world, and keep supporters informed and up-to-date.

Burma: BAT out of Burma!

In partnership with the Federation of Trade Unions – Burma

By 2003, British American Tobacco were one of the last multinationals to openly do business with the Burmese military dictatorship, a regime renowned for its appalling human rights record. BAT owned a cigarette factory in the military-owned Pyinmapin Industrial Zone. Their marketing was handled by a subsidiary of their military-controlled partners. Therefore, the IUF said, BAT was "directly and unambiguously involved with the ruling military dictatorship as joint venture partner, distributor and landlord."

Burma Campaign UK and the Federation of Trade Unions of Burma (FTUB) targeted BAT, whose deputy chairman at the time was senior British Conservative MP, Kenneth Clarke. Embarrassingly for the company, Clarke had described the Burmese regime as "totally contrary to our notions of civil liberties and democracy" in a letter to a constituent.

FTUB also received information that BAT was exporting fish products from the country in order to obtain foreign currency – using an industry notorious for its use of forced labour.

An international online campaign brought unions and NGOs around the world together, including Unison and Amicus (now Unite) in Britain, APHEDA in Australia, LabourStart, and the IUF.

In November 2003, BAT announced that it was selling its 60% share of its Burma-based subsidiary, after a formal request from the British government to do so. BAT said it left Burma 'with regret.'

Colombia: Banacol forced to honour contracts

In partnership with the International Union of Foodworkers

Colombia is one of the most dangerous places in the world to be a trade unionist. Many activists have been murdered by right-wing paramilitary groups during the country's long civil war. In 2004, Chiquita became the first US company to admit to making protection payments to one such militia, the AUC. That same year, the company faced lawsuits from three different groups of workers in Nicaragua and Costa Rica, for compensation because of exposure to various toxic chemicals.

Chiquita announced that it intended to sell its Colombian subsidiary, Banadex, in May 2004. The buyer, Colombian company Banacol, planned to turn permanent employees into contractors, which would have left them without union representation.

Banana union SINTRAINAGRO launched a 14-day strike, which LabourStart publicised at the request of the IUF. The strike ended on 10th June, having cost the employers $25 million. When the sale of Banadex went through the next day, Banacol agreed to uphold existing collective bargaining agreements, and award an 8% wage rise.

What We've Learned

LabourStart now has 15 years' experience of online campaigning in partnership with unions all over the world.

We know that online campaigns by themselves never lead to victory. The strongest online campaigns mentioned in this booklet were accompanied by lively campaigns on the ground. If there are strikes, pickets, rallies and imaginative protests to report, an online campaign will be more interesting, more frequently updated, and attract more people. If we have no progress to report, people will simply lose interest after a while.

The other side of the coin is that activists in the real world will feel more buoyed and confident if they know there is a strong online campaign behind them. Anyone who has been on a freezing cold picket line will tell you that it feels more worthwhile when someone stops by with a few words of solidarity. We can help bring solidarity from across the globe, and make sure that people know that ours is a truly international movement - it really does make a difference. If we can raise the morale of workers in a dispute enough that they stick at it for a while longer, that might be the time it takes for the bosses to cave in.

Some employers think they can get away with anything. Victimising and sacking people without compensation, breaching employment laws and ignoring court judgements, slashing wages and hours, going against contracts, and worse. They need to be forcefully reminded that the labour movement won't take it - that, as far as we're concerned, an injury to one is an injury to all.

We know that industrial disputes are ultimately won on the industrial battlefield. Public opinion is a secondary factor, but it is an important one. Many big companies are increasingly worried about their brand being seen to be "ethical." They often get away with things because they think no-one will know about it. Acting as a news service for trade unionists, keeping everyone up to date with struggles going on in other countries, is one way that LabourStart helps to stop this.

The other way is by mobilising public outrage against an employer. Obviously, certain employers are more susceptible to this than others. Big brands in the service industry, like Hilton, are more concerned with their public image than a garment factory owner in Bangladesh who you've never heard of. But what if that factory is making clothes for a big retail chain which has stores on every continent? Suddenly the campaign has a high profile target, another point on which to apply pressure.

This international nature of the global economy is often seen as being bad for workers, and of course it often is. But it is also potentially a source of great strength for us. It means that, when we enter into a struggle, we have allies all over the world - people who live thousands of miles away from each other but maybe work for the same boss. LabourStart is proudly internationalist, and that's why we work with a great network of volunteers to translate each of our campaigns into a dozen languages or more. Our campaigns our always international, always multilingual, and often run in partnership with one of the global union federations or the ITUC.

We believe that our experience and attitude makes us one of the global labour movement's most powerful online campaigning tools. This pamphlet serves as an introduction to some of the work we have done. Not every campaign is a success, or even a partial success. We are always learning, as the labour movement has always done, new and better ways of organising. But we have helped to achieve many victories by coupling the old principles of solidarity and internationalism with the new tools that the internet allows us to have at our disposal. We hope in the future to achieve many more.

What You Can Do

1. Sign up to all our current campaigns and sign up to new ones as they appear

You can sign up to our low-volume mailing list by clicking the link on the front page of our website www.labourstart.org

You'll also find a list of all our current active campaigns there for you to sign up to.

2. Spread the word about our campaigns to your friends, co-workers, and fellow union members

It's simple - the more people know about us, the bigger and more successful our campaigns will be. Make sure every union activist and community campaigner you know is aware of us and what we do. Direct people to our website, and the campaigns we run.

3. Use social networks such as Facebook and Twitter to amplify the message

Social media can help a campaign take off really quickly.

You can like and share our "LabourStart.org" Facebook page for all the latest news on the campaigns we run. Follow us on Twitter @labourstart. You can also join the LabourStart group on Linkedin, and sign up to unionbook.org, the social network for trade unionists.

4. Get your union to run our ActNOW campaigns newswire on its front page

Why not add one of our newswires to your union website? This allows your members to keep up to date with what's going on in the labour movement across the globe. Just add a line of code to your website, it's as easy as copy and paste!

The ActNOW newswire keeps all our current campaigns linked from your page:

www.labourstart.org/lnwcampaigns.shtml

And you can keep members up to date by adding one of our labour newswires, with national or international headlines updating every 15 minutes:

www.labourstart.org/lnwnews.shtml

5. Help us translate the campaigns into your local language

We rely on a network of volunteer translators to get the word out to as many people as possible. Our translators do fantastic work, and most of our campaign pages are available in about ten languages soon after they've launched. But we're always looking for more people to help. Contact ericlee@labourstart.org if you would like to volunteer.

6. Donate money to LabourStart to keep these campaigns going

We rely entirely on donations from the trade union movement. This pays for our office, staff, and web hosting costs. We accept regular donations via PayPal, from £2 per month up to whatever you're willing to give.

You can also buy our chosen Labour Book of the Month through our website, which helps fund us, as well as giving you an interesting read!

If you would like to advertise on our website, write to ericlee@labourstart.org.

7. Buy more copies of this book, and spread the word!

This book is available through Amazon in a number of countries. It's easy to order online - make sure your union branch has a copy.

Made in the USA
Charleston, SC
13 February 2013